Fish Hooks & Barbed Wire

Devotions for Country Folk

By Holly Hudson

Both fish hooks and barbed wire are extremely sharp and will cut you if you aren't careful. They can barely graze the skin and require only a bandage, or they can go deep and require a trip to the emergency room, or at least a friend who has watched a YouTube video.

The Word of God is also very sharp. As a matter of fact, it's sharper than any two-edged sword. It penetrates deep within the soul. Unlike the fish hook or barbed wire, this is a good thing. It's when God's Word goes deep that we are truly changed. I pray as you read these devotions and experiences from my childhood, and some more recent, that God's Word would penetrate your heart and transform you more and more into His likeness as you get to know Him better.

The Creek

No temptation has overtaken you that is not common to man. God is faithful, and He will not let you be tempted beyond your ability, but with the temptation He will also provide the way of escape, that you may be able to endure it. 1 Corinthians 10:13

Growing up, my family lived on a farm. Gran Gran had 30+ acres of farm land and we often helped work it at a young age. Regardless, we had a huge playground on which to run and play. We were allowed to go anywhere between our house and the creek but couldn't go past the creek if Mommy or Daddy weren't with us. We loved the creek and spent most of our time fishing, sliding down the tiny waterfall and just sitting and enjoying the quiet. There was a big rock that hung over the creek. I always called it "my rock" and I would spend time talking with Jesus while gazing at His awesome creation. It was a fun place to play but I sometimes wonder if one of the reasons we loved being there so much was because it was as far as we were allowed to go without getting in trouble. Although there was nothing bad on the other side, it could be exciting to push the limits. I know my parents made the rule because they loved us. The rule was meant to keep us safe and to also have less area to cover if they came looking for us.

As Christians, there are lines that shouldn't be crossed. It may be what we watch, hear, say, or do. Often like little kids, we walk the property line of what's right and wrong. The danger is real on the other side as well as on the line. When we are on the line, the temptation is so much harder to resist. Most of the time, it's the curiosity of what's on the other side that grips us. Although we have the power in Christ to resist any temptation, we shouldn't make it more difficult on ourselves. For example, if I'm craving a brownie and there are no brownies in my house, it's pretty easy to resist. However, if brownies are coming out of the oven, the temptation is real and hard to resist. I take one bite and before they're even cool, the entire pan is gone.

God gives us limits for our good. He loves us and our identity is in Him. The limits are not a punishment but are meant to help us be who He made us to be. God also gives us grace and mercy if we've crossed that line once or more times than we can count. There is forgiveness and grace upon grace. He will clothe you with Christ and make you holy and blameless if you ask.

Next time you are tempted to walk the property line, rely on His perfect strength through prayer and His promises to keep you far from the line.

Watch Your Step

You gave a wide place for my steps under me, and my feet did not slip. 2 Samuel 22:37

My great aunt's property joined Gran Gran's at the creek. There was a fishing pond on her property and we loved to spend the day fishing with my family. One on occasion, my cousins were visiting so my dad decided to take us fishing at the pond. There were five of us, so we walked the 60 acres carrying our rods and tackle. Along the way, there were barbed wire fences that we had to cross. This was nothing new to me and JJ, but my cousins weren't as accustomed to it. Daddy helped us by holding one cable down with his boot and held the other up with his hand so we could get through safely. After we were all on the other side, he stepped over and lost his footing, landing face first on the barbed wire. His cuts were deep and should have cancelled our fishing trip, but he didn't. He took us fishing and then went to the emergency room for stitches later.

We quickly learned that it's important to watch your step in a pasture. Some of the dangers that could be encountered are holes, slick spots, briars, snakes and of course cow patties. It's very important to avoid the last one.

In the Christian life, we must be careful and intentional where we step. There are numerous land mines waiting to detonate and destroy our lives. We may not even know we have an issue until we step on it. Some of those land mines could be watching explicit scenes in a movie (or a commercial for that matter), having a drink with friends, spending too much time alone with your boyfriend, or spending time with the wrong friends. The list is endless and it's different for each of us.

So how do we avoid these seemingly invisible land mines? We must bathe ourselves daily in the Word of God, so we can hear His voice and follow in His footsteps, so we don't lose our footing. When we do step away from Jesus' footprints, and we will, He is there to pull us back to our feet and cover the sin with the bandage of His blood. He forgives and remembers our sin no more.

Ask Jesus to be your Guide and light your path today and every day.

Digging Worms

This Book of the Law shall not depart from your mouth, but you shall meditate on it day and night, so that you may be careful to do according to all that is written in it. For then you will make your way prosperous, and then you will have good success. Joshua 1:8

As children, and even now, we loved to fish. There were many times we would run out of bait. This was no problem for us because there was an unlimited supply in the ditch beside our house. Sometimes digging for worms was just as fun as catching fish.

The ditch was always covered with leaves because that's where we dumped the leaves after raking. We found bait as we raked back the leaves. One of us would rake and the others would collect the worms in a can. However, we would find the most and biggest worms when we used the shovel to dig deeper. There were so many worms that the kid with the shovel had to help gather them before they crawled back into the earth.

Reading God's Word is kind of like digging worms. We see a lot of truth on the surface by reading a passage. However, to get to know Him more intimately, sometimes we need a shovel to dig deeper. Some of the shovels we can use are other translations, meditating on the passage, praying, listening to God, etc. When we spend this extra time and effort, He shows us more of Himself and His Word becomes part of us. I encourage you to dig deep and let His Spirit teach your heart and deepen your relationship with Him.

Night Fishing

Jesus said to Him, "I am the way, and the Truth, and the Life. No one comes to the Father except through me." John 14:6

One of my favorite activities at The Lake was night fishing as a child. It was so much fun and a great time to be with the entire family. Everyone fished, from the youngest to the oldest.

Just before dark we would start getting ready. We made sure everyone had a rod and reel with the appropriate gold crappie hook and sinker. My rod was green with a Zebco 202 reel. It was a birthday gift from Uncle Freddy and Aunt Rhonda. They always bought us the coolest gifts.

A minnow run was the next item on the agenda. A few of us would take the pontoon to "The Camp" just around the bend to get eight dozen or so minnows. It was better to have too many than not enough if the fish started biting. The

Camp, called Skippers Landing, was a landing that my Granddaddy and Grandmother Hill built and owned when my mother was little. Mom told me stories of Grandmother cleaning and cooking the fish that the fisherman would catch. At that time, it was called "Hill's Camp." Therefore, it will always be known as "The Camp" to us.

Uncle Freddy and Daddy filled the lanterns with kerosene and put new wicks on them and started pumping. I thought that was so cool as I watched them prepare the lanterns. The more they pumped, the brighter they became.

Now, to find enough chairs for the number of people who wanted to go. The list usually included: Mom, Daddy, JJ and me; Freddy and Rhonda; Leon, Brian, Stevie and Amy; Ernest and Ernie; and Grandmother. We didn't have those cool bag chairs back then, so we gathered all the folding chairs we could find and even a kitchen chair or two. We lined the chairs up on the right side of the pontoon because that's where the lanterns would be. The other side of the pontoon contained the minnows, fish bucket, life jackets and ice chest with drinks and snacks.

The pontoon was a basic fishing model. The rails were a faded red with an old Johnson motor on the back. It had one captain's chair, if you could call it that. Most importantly, there was plenty of room, which is very important when you have 10 to 15 people fishing.

About dusk, we would pile on and ride out to one of our favorite crappie spots. We left that to Uncle Freddy. He always seemed to know the best fishing spots. When the anchors were lowered and the lanterns were safely attached to the hooks hanging over the side, we would "bait up" and take our assigned positions. Yes, even on a pontoon everyone had their spot. Mine was near the front inside the rail beside the lantern. This proved to always be a lucrative spot for fishing and yes, for bugs and spiders. One thing I failed to mention was the amount of OFF that was used. We not only sprayed ourselves from head to toe, but also as much of the pontoon as we could. There are two ways to put a minnow on your hook without killing it. Fish bite better if the bait is wiggling. The first way is to hook it through the upper lip and the second is just below the fin. We didn't need to use corks because the fish were below us in the brush pile above which we were anchored. One of the most important things was to remember how many "pulls," or how deep you were if you caught something. A pull is grabbing your line at the reel and pulling to the first eye of the rod. Crappies tend to stay together in a school. The first thing that everyone wanted to know when the first crappie was caught was "how many pulls?" Then everyone winds in their line and adjusts their depth to match the number of "pulls."

We would stay out there until about 1:00 or 2:00am and catch maybe 50 or 60 nice crappie. When some of us kids would get tired, we would fall asleep on the cushy life jackets in the floor. We knew it was time to go in when the fish stopped biting, or we ran out of minnows. My cousins, my brother and I huddled around the lanterns for warmth as we headed toward the house.

We were tired when we got back but the fish still had to be cleaned. The men took care of that by the lantern's light while we went inside to get storage bags to put the fish in after they had been cleaned.

There were a lot of late nights, but some of the best family fun that I remember as a child. Everyone (young and old) was together and enjoying one another's company. There were lots of laughs and lots of fish.

I miss those times on the lake late at night. That's one of my favorite times to be out on the water. The lake is as smooth as glass with nothing but the moon to illuminate the way. Even today, when I'm at the lake, I enjoy being on the lake at night. The best time is when the moon is full and you can see where you're going. A boat doesn't have head lights, so we rely on various lights along the way to guide the journey. It may be the light at The Camp that shows where to turn or a light on a neighbor's pier that helps guide us. Those little lights seem really bright when it's the darkest, but it's always easier if the big light in the sky is leading the way.

It's the same with our lives. Jesus is the light and in Him there is no darkness. We can attempt to follow little lights, the lights of others, but we will never find the way; or we can follow the True Light of Jesus, who is the Way. Let us fix our eyes on Him and glide into that everlasting home that He's prepared for those who have a relationship with Him.

The Front Porch

And rising very early in the morning, while it was still dark, He departed and went out to a desolate place, and there He prayed. Mark 1:35

My dream house is a house on the lake with a rocking chair front porch. Why? Because of the front porch at the lake. On the lake, the front porch is the one facing the lake, not the road. There was really nothing that special about the porch. It had a swing on one end and a variety of chairs lined the remaining portions. It was my favorite place to go when I woke up early in the morning. The lake was so peaceful and only Grandmother and I would be awake. She and I would sit on that porch swing and enjoy one another's company as we looked across the lake. She was one of my favorite people, and I think of her every time I sit on that swing.

By 9:00am, the porch would be full of people. I'm not sure how that old porch withstood the weight of that many people, but it did. Some people only left the porch to sleep and eat.

Some wouldn't even leave to do that. There was something about that porch that helped us escape from all the worries of the world. Some of my best "quiet times" (time with the Lord) were on that porch. Looking back, I know it was because there were few distractions and He could have my full attention.

It's nice to have a place like the lake to spend time with Jesus, but we can spend time with Him wherever we are. It is a conscious decision to find a quiet place and turn off distractions so we can hear His voice. Often for me, that time comes as I drive to work or go for a walk, but I can find that time at home as well if I'll make it a priority. His desire to spend time with us should be all the motivation we need.

Battle Scars

For we do not wrestle against flesh and blood, but against the rulers, against the authorities, against the cosmic powers over this present darkness, against the spiritual forces of evil in the heavenly places. **Ephesians 6:12**

Even though it was many years ago, the memory of the Eagles and Cobras won't be forgotten. These were two clubs that my cousins, brother and I formed during our summers. Our time together at the lake consisted of many battles, which would sometimes leave scars. Looking back, I cannot claim either team as my own. We didn't know who would constitute each team from one day to the next. Membership was often determined by events that took place the previous day. If a teammate said or did something to make us angry, the teams would be reorganized.

Our clubs had secret passwords and meeting places, which the other team always managed to know. For this reason, the passwords were subject to change. Our meeting places (club houses) were generally one of two places: either under the house or on the pontoon. My favorite was under the house. It was there that we found our weapons and mapped out our battle plans.

Yes, battle plans. This was the primary activity in which the teams engaged, and our battle plans included the use of weapons. The badminton rackets we found under the house made perfect guns to fire our bullets, which were those porky-pine looking "gumballs" that fall from the trees. On the defensive, our life jackets served as bulletproof vests. Our ships were twelve foot john boats guided by paddles or trolling motors. The only thing missing was protection for our faces, which caused even worse fights. If someone was hit in the face, he or she began to fight with even more passion. This usually turned what had started as a game into a real fight. One of these battles almost ended in a disaster.

We were in one of our typical battles when we decided to move it to the dock. Steve was on the pier, so we let Brian out on the pier as well. Ernie and I were watching from the boat and JJ was on the bank. As Brian and Steve were fighting, they moved out to the front of the pontoon, which was tied to the dock. Before I knew what had happened, Brian had been pushed into the lake. It wouldn't have been that big of deal, except it was Easter vacation. The air temperature was in the sixties, which meant the water was extremely cold. I had always heard that if someone falls into extremely cold water, they can't move. I was seeing this first hand at the age of ten. Brian looked like a huge cork bobbing up and down with the waves. He couldn't even speak. His mouth seemed to be frozen shut. However, he did communicate to me with his eyes. Unlike his mouth, his eyes were opened wide. I saw fear and helplessness as our eyes met. He was calling out for help without a word. He was very fortunate to be wearing his life jacket because it took me a while to know what to do.

Ernie quickly paddled over to where Brian was in the water. I held out my hand to him, but his did not reach out to me. I had to get him out of that water fast. Without thinking, I grabbed the back of his life vest with both hands. I pulled him halfway into the boat with his stomach resting on the side. Since his legs were now, for the most part, out of the water, he was able to lift one over the side. We immediately took him into the house, where he got out of his wet clothes and we were interrogated by our parents. I don't remember if we were punished or not. The traumatic experience was punishment enough for me to learn my lesson.

We look back to those days and laugh at the things we did. No one was ever seriously injured during our battles. This incident was probably the most serious. Those were the "good ole days." We had no real responsibilities and spent a lot of time together. Today, we only see each other on special occasions because we are so busy with life. The days of our youth seemed stressful at the time, but sometimes I wish the war between the Cobras and Eagles never had to end. Those were some of the best days that I have ever had at the lake. Those times will never be forgotten.

Today we face other battles. Sometimes we can see our opponent and other times our opponent is hidden. Recently, I went through a season of intense spiritual warfare. It was like nothing I had ever faced and I know it had to be spiritual because the weight was heavy and continued to push me down. I had trouble sleeping and had weird dreams when I did. I walked around defeated and needed relief but couldn't describe the problem and therefore didn't know how to fight it. I was so exhausted that I couldn't even find the strength to pray, so often my prayers consisted of one word - "Jesus." He knew what I needed even though I couldn't find the words. Finally, I asked a dear friend to pray over me. I think it was a little weird for her but she felt God leading her to do this. As she prayed, the weight lifted and a peace came over me that I hadn't felt in some time. Praying for and with other believers is so important to fight the enemy. Make intercessory prayer a priority and you won't believe the strength He will give you. A spiritual battle requires a spiritual solution. Let God fight these battles as you look to Him for victory.

A 4th of July Tradition

Your word is a lamp to my feet and a light to my path. Psalm 119:105

I remembered talking about the tradition that my uncles and older cousins started at the lake many years ago. Every year on July 4th they would build a pyramid on waterskis. I don't recall ever seeing them do this but saw it in the Polaroid they took. I remember telling my friends what they used to do and thinking how awesome it must have been.

One year while I was in college I went to the lake a little earlier than my parents. When I walked onto the front porch, Uncle Freddy inquired as to who would revive the tradition. At that age, I would try anything once, and so we went to Lowe's to pick up the necessary items to "the bar." The bar was one of the most important pieces of the puzzle. It had to float but also had to be able to withstand the pressure of three skiers getting up behind a bass boat. We purchased PVC pipe, a broom handle and a sturdy rope. I watched Uncle

Freddy as he slid the broom handle inside the pipe and drilled holes for the rope. When he was finished constructing what was now our ski rope, he laid it against the rail on the porch. Mom and Dad came down that evening and walked on the porch – that's the first thing all of us do when we get to the lake. As mom sat down, her eyes were fixed on "the bar." She knew but she asked anyway, "What's that?" I told her it was the pyramid bar. She knew the answer to her next question as well, "And who is going to be on top?" I looked at her with a huge smile. Her response, "That's what I was afraid of." She had seen many of these done, but none with her little girl on top of the pyramid.

I began to understand her concern the following morning as we began to practice on land. The instructions must be followed exactly or someone could get hurt. Each of us, my uncle, my brother and myself, all started out on two skis. They used the old, wooden Cypress Garden skis because they were wide and could hold more weight. I had two slaloms. Now, it had been a long time since any of us had skied on two skis, so I knew we would be a little out of practice, but that wasn't the main concern. I found out that I would have to drop both skis as we drove by the dock. I had dropped a ski before. That's how I learned how to slalom, but I had much rather get up on one. It's so much easier. After I dropped the right ski, I was to put my foot on the back of one of theirs and proceed to do the same with the other. Once both feet were resting on the back of their skies, I then would start climbing. They would squat and I was to grab whatever I needed to grab to make my way to their shoulders while the boat was pulling us. Once I reached the top, my uncle would then hand me my rope and an American Flag as we circled the cove. The most important instruction was DO NOT FALL FORWARD! He went on to explain that if I fell forward they would run over me with their skies. I didn't want to fall period and wasn't sure if I fell that I could control how. However, I was young and wasn't too concerned. How hard can it be? These are often the five words that get me in the most trouble.

The family stood on the dock as we began our task. My grandmother was right there with them to watch and give instructions. As I began to climb on our first try, I leaned forward and as I fell, hooked my brother's leg and he did a hard nose dive. The second time, I leaned back and fell off backwards as I climbed. This is when I started praying that the Lord would help me do it right this time because Uncle Freddy said one more time. Because of my competitive nature, I knew I wouldn't rest until I succeeded. I was reminded of one of the instructions I was given – grab whatever you need to in order to keep your balance and ascend to the top. On our final try, I used their heads/hair to balance myself and made my way to the top. As I reached for the rope, I ripped the flag from my uncle's mouth and held it high in victory. That was so much fun and something I'll always remember.

The instructions we were given as we built the pyramid were to help us accomplish our goal but also to keep us safe. It's the same with the Word of God. The Lord gives us instructions, not to limit us, but to help us safely achieve the potential we have because of Him. It's when we try things our own way that we fall, and often times experience devastating hurt and sadness. Let His Word be your guiding light as you travel through this life. He has your best interest at heart.

Slow Fishing

He makes me lie down in green pastures. He leads me beside still waters. Psalm 23:2

Just the other day my uncle told me the story of how Daddy caught his big fish. It was spring of the year and they were fishing along the bank and my uncle saw a muddy spot and told Daddy to cast there. When he cast, the fish took the bait but Daddy missed it. He threw in the same spot once more, and this time he landed a 10 pound largemouth bass. Dad never caught very many bass but when he did, he caught big ones. I think it's because he fished slow. He'd make a cast and it would take him thirty minutes to drag that worm across the bottom of the lake and back to the boat. Big bass generally like to look at their dinner before eating and they sometimes take a good hard look, so fishermen who aren't patient generally do not bring in the big catch.

I can learn a lot from my dad. He didn't get in a hurry, but I'm always in a hurry. If we take the time to catch the fish, so to speak, our reward is great. We catch the beauty God has painted for us in His creation. That beauty comes in many different forms. I love being at the lake late in the evening or early in the morning. The masterpieces He gives us are breath-taking but if I'm in my race, I miss it.

Another thing we miss is those we love. When I'm busy, I try to fit others into my schedule and often spend that time looking at my phone trying to get to my next appointment. That's not beautiful quality time. We must slow down or miss glimpses of our Savior. He tells us to be still. He even makes us lie down in green pastures because He knows we need that rest. When I have continued to resist lying down in His rest, He usually gets my attention in ways I don't prefer. I'll get sick and have to slow down or get so run down that I can't fulfill my schedule. Slow down and meet with Him wherever you are. He is there waiting on us so that we can be refreshed and have strength to face the next challenge.

Biscuits

Each of you should use whatever gift you have received to serve others, as faithful stewards of God's grace in its various forms. 1 Peter 4:10

It's a typical Saturday morning at the lake. I'm still in the bed when I hear pans rattling in the kitchen. It's only seven o'clock but I'm afraid to close my eyes because I know exactly what's going on in the kitchen. The best thing for me to do is to get up so I won't miss the thing I've been waiting for since the last time we were at the lake.

I look over and see that Mom's still asleep and my dad is not there. I also notice that my brother isn't on the bottom bunk. I guess they decided to go fishing early this morning. I hope the fishing trip is profitable. Unless they get back shortly, they are going to miss the happenings in the kitchen.

As I enter the kitchen, there she is busily at work, not noticing that she's no longer alone. I watch her as she gets out her rolling pin and dusts it with flour. She looks up as I get some Dr. Pepper from the refrigerator and says, "Good morning" with a warm smile. She then proceeds with her endeavor. She carefully pours the buttermilk over the clump of lard in the center of the mounted flour. The dough runs smoothly through her fingers, and before long the dough is no longer wet. As she kneads the dough, it begins to look much more appealing than it did when she began.

Now she rolls the dough out onto the table, making the lump of dough even. After doing this, she proceeds to cut the biscuits with the red biscuit cutter. I've never seen her use any other one. Yes! There's a piece of leftover dough. I've always loved to eat biscuit dough, especially hers. She takes the remainder in her hand and makes it into a big biscuit and says, "This one's mine!" In the oven they go.

The anticipation is mounting. Maybe they'll get done more quickly if I watch them through the glass door on the oven. I watch for about a minute but it feels like a lifetime. I'll just get ready so I'll be prepared when she takes them

out of the oven. I get the butter and jelly out of
the refrigerator and set them on the table.
They taste the best when they are smothered
with butter while they're hot. My knife is
ready, as a matter of fact, it's in my hand.

I'm startled as I hear the over door open. Could
they be ready? Grandmother picks one up with
her bare hand to see if it's brown enough on
the bottom. They're not quite ready, rats!
After what seems like years of anticipation, she
takes them out of the stove and we begin to
butter them. I'm not that patient, so I eat one
while buttering the others.

One by one I hear doors opening and, as I look
down the hall, I see a line for the bathroom.
Everyone is anxious. It's not that they need to
get into the bathroom, they just want to get
into the kitchen before everyone else. Some
postpone going to the bathroom in order to get
into the kitchen quicker. Once everyone's in
the kitchen, each person is on his own. If you
want a biscuit, you grab it. Don't expect anyone
to pass you one.

Everyone's quiet, which is extremely unusual for my family. As I look around the room, I can see a resemblance on the face of each one - a smile. That's kind of strange considering it's so early on a Saturday morning. Most people are still asleep at this time. Grandmother is sitting by herself in a corner admiring her masterpiece. She has created an unbelievable amount of happiness with her own hands. I can't express with words the joy she receives in doing things for her family. She doesn't get up that early to make biscuits for herself; she has us in mind.

I hear a boat speeding toward the house. It's probably JJ and Dad coming in from fishing. I look at the table and there's one biscuit left. We could leave it there and let them fight over it; or eat it so they'll never know it was there. Actually they probably will know because everyone's awake and in the kitchen. We leave it, which is rather cruel. As they come in, they are talking about what they caught and the one that got away. Then their eyes shift to the table. Before a word can be said, it's consumed by my brother. My dad tries to hide his disappointment, but Grandmother can see beyond his jokes. Even though he's only her son-in-law, she begins cooking bacon and eggs for him. He's content with the substitute but would rather have the hot buttery biscuit that JJ so quickly grabbed. Next time he'll wait until after breakfast to go fishing or take Grandmother with him.

This is one of the many stories that shows Grandmother's servant heart. Ever since I can remember, she has always done things for other people while putting her own interests on hold.

Like a rock, she is solid and rarely changing. We can lean on her and trust that she'll hold us. But if we happen to fall, she'll go down with us. If there was ever a person in my life who portrayed a Christ-like character, it's her. I can see Christ's love in everything she does, which makes her even more special.

She has had a tremendous impact on my life. Ever since I was a little girl, I have admired her. She never seems to look to her own interest because others are more important. In looking at her example, I have come to enjoy doing things for others. I love to see the smile on someone's face when I go out of my way to help them. Even though I'll probably never be as self-sacrificing as Grandmother, I often do sacrifice my time in order to bring a little happiness to someone else.

One day I was talking with someone and she told me that I reminded her of my Grandmother. I cannot begin to express the way I felt at that time. I guess it was a combination of pride and humility. I was proud to be associated with her because of her greatness. It also humbled me because I knew that I would never be as special as she is. I saw it as an unattainable feat. I'm not saying that I'm not like Grandmother. It's just hard to look in a mirror and see something good.

When I look back at Grandmother's strength in different situations, I see the same source of power in her that I've had in me during trials in my life. Jesus has always been a major part of our lives, and it isn't until difficult situations that I realize the greatness of His strength. He is the source of incomparable strength and as His children we have access to an unlimited amount of strength and perseverance.

Now, when I look back to the time when I was compared to my Grandmother I am filled with joy. I now realize that what that person saw in me that reminded her of Grandmother was Jesus Christ. I feel proud because I know Jesus and He evidentially does shine through me. However, I am humbled because I have so far to go to be transformed into His image.

I'm so thankful for Grandmother and the example she has been not only to me, but to many others. As she now lives with her King, I'll continue to persevere until He calls me home as well.

Tree Pruning

He cuts off every branch in me that bears no fruit, while every branch that does bear fruit he prunes so that it will be even more fruitful.
John 15:2

I remember one spring it was so warm, and I love skiing so much, I begged and begged to go skiing. My parents both agreed that the water was too cold to go skiing, so I pouted. My dad had a better idea. He wanted me to help him trim limbs so he could see the lake more clearly from the porch. We have one of the biggest water oaks on the front that I've ever seen. The limbs are so big and heavy that they often hang down so low that our view is obstructed. This is how we trimmed the limbs. Dad would find a long rope and tie some heavy bolts, washers or whatever he could find to the end of the rope. He would then loop the rope several times and hold that portion in his left hand while he tossed the heavy end up and over the limb he wanted to cut. Using both feet as leverage, he would pull the limb as far down as he could. Often, he would almost be on the ground trying to hold it in place. My brother or I would

proceed to hook the limb with the pole pruner
as high as we could and cut the limb. Yes,
sometimes the limb would fall on us, so we had
to be aware and get out of the way. We would
spend hours cutting limbs and instead of
burning the limbs, sometimes we would make a
bed for the fish. All the limbs were piled
together, and rope was weaved in and out of
the limbs to hold them together and tied to a
few blocks to serve as anchors. Finally, it was
time to put the brush pile in the lake. We did
this in different ways. Often, we used the boat
or pontoon to drag it out to the spot we wanted
to drop it. However, this time my dad wanted
to put it on the edge of the point just off shore.
Dad had said we couldn't go skiing but wading
in the water to pull it out to the perfect spot
was acceptable. He kept tell me to go out
further and further. As I followed his
instructions, eventually I was completely over
my head and had to go under to get traction on
the bottom of the lake to pull it to the perfect
spot. To this day, I still don't understand why it
was fine to pull that brush pile out but too cold
to go skiing.

Going back to the reason we started this
endeavor, we find great truth. Dad didn't want

an obstructed view of the lake. The lake is beautiful and brings great peace as we fix our gaze on it. When the limbs are hanging down, we don't see it as clearly.

There are many things that obstruct our view of Jesus. Sin is at the top of the list, but sometimes it's seemingly good things that get in the way as well. Our activities, our relationships with others and our attitudes are just few. We must continually evaluate our lives and our hearts to see if anything is getting in the way of our relationship with Jesus. When those things are revealed to us, it's necessary to reprioritize and sometimes prune those things in our lives. Sometimes it's a lot of work and unpleasant especially when we don't understand what exactly He's doing in our lives. We may even find ourselves over our head at times. But when we get to the place we can sit and relax on the porch, so to speak, we will gaze upon the beauty of the Lord and it will all be worth it.

Ask the Lord what areas need reprioritizing and what areas need pruning. His beauty and His peace are worth the sacrifice.

Site Fishing

She gave this name to the LORD who spoke to her: "You are the God who sees me," for she said, "I have now seen the One who sees me." Genesis 16:13

I went site fishing for the first time a few years ago with my brother. Site fishing is what you do when the bass are spawning. They make their bed by fanning out the spot with their tail. You can usually find them by spotting the cleared out area with shells marking it. Sounds pretty simple but it isn't. There are a few essentials to be successful site fishing, but the most important is polarized shades. These are necessary to see the bottom of the lake more clearly. Even with my shades on, I still had trouble finding the fish. My brother saw the bass much more clearly than I did and he caught some good ones. After casting at numerous bedding fish, I finally caught one. It was a lot of fun but being able to see the fish made the difference. With an experienced site fisherman, the bass are at a huge disadvantage. They are vulnerable to being caught, hurt and maybe fried and eaten.

Vulnerability is something that scares most of us. We fear others seeing the "real" us and being hurt. People can be fickle. We have a God who has something better than polarized glasses. Our God is a God who sees us. He not only sees what we do, but He also sees who we really are – our thoughts, dreams, insecurities, sins, and the things we don't want anyone to see. He sees the good stuff, but He also sees the ugly junk in our hearts. When I think about this at the surface, it's scary. Why would He love me based on what He sees? As I look deeper into the character of God, I see a God who loves me unconditionally and works things together for my good – even the bad stuff. Deep down, we all want someone to know us intimately and love us for who we are and not for what we can do for them or who we pretend to be. We have that Friend in Jesus. He sees me, He loves me, He accepts me…. No questions asked.

Smoky

If we confess our sins, he is faithful and just and will forgive us our sins and purify us from all unrighteousness. 1 John 1:9

When I was a little girl, I loved horses. I didn't have one of my own, but I had neighbors who did, and I would occasionally get to ride. My cousin had a pony that we would jump on bareback and hang onto his mane until he ran against a tree or fence and knocked us to the ground. My senior year of high school my dad bought a horse. His name was Smoky, which fit his appearance. He was a smoky gray quarter horse. I loved Smoky and rode him often that summer. One day as I enjoyed a run across the field with my buddy, he saw the barn and turned quickly and almost tossed me. I was able to stay mounted and stop him. At that point I could have given in to the fear of being thrown off or continue riding. I didn't want Smoky to think he was in control, so I jumped off, tightened the saddle and continued to enjoy my ride.

When it comes to sin, we will all fall like I almost did from my horse. The important thing is that we get back up. We can't let our failures define our lives. As Christians, we have the power of the Holy Spirit living in us. He will give us the strength to resist when temptation comes in the future if we will look to him. Next time you fall, look to Jesus for forgiveness and the power to resist it in the future. Sin has no power over us.

I'm Not a Doctor, but I Saw it on YouTube

He heals the brokenhearted and binds up their wounds. Psalm 147:3

My brother, JJ, was fishing with my cousin, Steve. Steve had caught a striper and was attempting to remove the treble hook when the fish flopped and threw the hook into Steve's thumb. It was deep, and an emergency room trip was their next stop.

However, my brilliant little brother said he had seen this video on YouTube and assured Steve that he could remove it. The procedure involved wrapping fishing line around the hook and jerking it out. Steve wasn't so sure but decided to let JJ give it a try. I think they were both astonished that the trick JJ saw on the video worked so well.

Some injuries require a doctor and others do not. The same is true for our emotional injuries. Some things are minor, like not being invited to a gathering. This can often be remedied by talking to a friend or eating some ice cream. I have some friends who have been the victim of some serious physical and emotional hurts. Even being left out can become serious if it continues to happen or we don't deal with it. The scars can only be healed by a specialist. No, I'm not talking about a psychologist, although they can help.

Ultimately, the only one who can truly heal these hurts is the Great Physician. Our Lord knows our past, the things we've endured, and He can heal them. There was a time I went to a Christian counselor who helped me deal with the death of my father. With her help, I recognized the pain and was able to take it to the Lord, who continues to heal my sadness.

Regardless of what you've been through, take those hurts to the Lord. He loves you and in His presence is safety and great healing.

Trash or Treasure

He will rescue them from oppression and violence, for precious is their blood in His sight. Psalm 72:14

When I was a kid, we spent a lot of fall Saturday mornings driving from one yard sale to another. Mom would map out the ones she wanted to go to the previous night so we could hit the best ones first. We didn't have a lot of material things growing up. Most of my clothes were from yard sales or hand me downs from my cousins. She loved yard sales, but I didn't enjoy going through boxes and boxes of clothes to find something that would fit and that I liked. However, as I glanced over the junk, I would sometimes find that one treasure - the item I couldn't afford at the store but really wanted. One man's trash is often another man's treasure. This is true in life as well.

Each one of us has felt like or been treated like trash at one time or another. Unkind words or looks have a huge impact on how we view ourselves. In some cases, the abuse is physical or emotional. Regardless, we leave feeling worthless and begin to label ourselves as such.

But that is a lie from Satan! We are worth more than we can imagine to our Heavenly Father. He said and demonstrated that we are worth Jesus. We are His treasure, His love, His beautiful bride. Next time you feel ugly, fat, undesirable or like common trash, remember that you are a treasure worth the very life of Jesus. He paid the ultimate price, so He could have fellowship with you. He desires you and wants you to know how truly valuable you are.

Tomatoes

The law was brought in so that the trespass might increase. But where sin increased, grace increased all the more, so that, just as sin reigned in death, so also grace might reign through righteousness to bring eternal life through Jesus Christ our Lord. Romans 5:20,21

My Gran Gran worked harder than anyone I know. She spent her work days picking up eggs at the local chicken farm and her evenings and Saturdays working her garden. I didn't realize how big her garden was until she became sick and asked me to plant tomatoes. She made sure I did it correctly and watched me very closely. I had to pour a dipper of water on each one after covering the roots. I worked for hours planting and finally decided to count them. She had 98 tomato plants. When I asked her why she needed so many, she said someone else may need some. You can't have too many and she gave many tomatoes and other vegetables to others.

That's right, GAVE. She didn't plant them to sell but wanted to bless others.

The same is true about God's grace. Grace is God's unmerited favor. There is nothing you can do to earn it. It's free and you can't have too much. One of my favorite passages about His grace is Romans 5:20. My paraphrase: you can't out-sin God's grace. In other words, regardless of what you've done, God's grace through the work of Jesus is sufficient to cover it all. This isn't a license to sin but forgiveness for the one who recognizes their sin, confesses it to the Lord and turns from it. This doesn't mean we will never fall into that sin again but does mean that we are not living in sin.

Since we have been given so much, we should extend grace to others as well. Instead we become judgmental and save our grace for certain people, unlike God's grace. He lavishes grace on anyone who will receive it. Be an instrument of His grace. He's forgiven us so much, how can we not forgive others?

Stay on the Path

Enter through the narrow gate. For wide is the gate and broad is the road that leads to destruction, and many enter through it. But small is the gate and narrow is the road that leads to life, and only a few find it. Matthew 7:13,14

I enjoyed living next door to my grandparents. A hayfield separated our house from theirs. When we cut grass, we always cut the path to their house as well. Sometimes the grass on either side of the path was so tall that all mom could see was two blond heads bobbing up and down as we ran down to Gran Gran's. We traveled that path every day because we loved going to her house. As often as we walked and rode our bikes down the path, I'm surprised it even needed to be cut. One thing is for sure, we didn't veer off the path often. When we did, we would fall off our bikes or be itchy from the grass hitting our legs. We decided it was best to stay on the path.

God talks about two paths – the narrow and wide roads. The wide road leads to destruction but the narrow road leads to life. How do you know if you're on the right road? Test it with scripture. If what you are doing is contrary to the Word of God, you've taken the wrong road. There is a narrow gate at the beginning of the road that leads to life. The gate is Jesus. It's only through Him that we are allowed on the path that leads to life and freedom. He cleanses us from the sin that has led us down the wrong path for so long. Seek the narrow path and enter through Jesus to an everlasting, joyful life in Him.

The Big Orange Cork

Do not conform to the pattern of this world, but be transformed by the renewing of your mind. Then you will be able to test and approve what God's will is – His good, pleasing and perfect will.

Romans 12:2

One Christmas my brother and cousin were talking about how good the fish were biting and somehow talked me into going with them. I am what they call a "fair weather fisherman." In other words, I like to fish when it's sunny and 70, not when it's cold and rainy. This particular day it was going to be very cold and windy, not to mention my brother only knows one speed while driving the boat, which makes it even colder. The warmest thing I could find was an orange puffy hunting jumpsuit. They laughed and laughed at me, saying I looked like a big orange cork. Even though I was a bit embarrassed, I wore that hideous jumpsuit because it kept me relatively warm as we fished. I think they told me a fish story because we didn't get one bite.

When I think about how I stood out in that outfit, I think about how different we should look than those who don't know Christ. We have a joy and a hope that should shine through us like a flood light giving light to all those around us. Too often we are scared to be or look different, so we attempt to blend in so we don't draw attention to ourselves. However, the warmth we have in Christ is worth the stares and maybe just one of those people staring will want what we have – Jesus. So next time you're embarrassed because you're not like everyone else, remember you are called to be different.

Styrofoam Boat

Therefore, confess your sins to each other and pray for each other so that you may be healed. The prayer of a righteous person is powerful and effective. James 5:16

As children with a lot of time and energy on our hands, sometimes we had to be creative when we were at the lake. Most of our treasures were found in the damp dirt floor basement. One year we found huge pieces of Styrofoam that were used to ship refrigerators. We put the hollow end on the water and sat on the solid end with our feet hanging off the side. By adding a long handled paddle, we had a boat. We paddled all over our swimming area. Thinking back, I wonder what people thought when they saw us. When we weren't using it as a boat, it became a clubhouse since the underneath side was hollow. We could go under the boat and actually breathe and be out of sight at the same time. We thought it awesome. We were like two-year old's who play with a box rather than the toy.

As adults, we enjoy hiding as well. We wear masks so others can't see the real us. But God created us for fellowship with Him and others. We're a lot like Adam and Eve, who hid from the One who knows all. His desire is for us to cry out to Him, confess and ask for His help. He loves us so much despite the sin we are trying to hide. He wants to restore us but if we keep suppressing these things, it'll make us sick – physically, emotionally and spiritually. Cry out to Jesus. He's waiting to listen and wrap His loving, forgiving arms around us.

He has also given us others to encourage and pray for us. When we hide from those closest to us, we miss out on the fellowship, encouragement and prayers that they can offer. It's important to have a few close Christian friends in whom you can confide even your deepest hurts and sins. Let's spend more time on top of the Styrofoam boat and less time hiding underneath.

I Am Not Ashamed

For I am not ashamed of the gospel, because it is the power of God that brings salvation to everyone who believes; first to the Jew, then to the Gentile. Romans 1:16

I love sports, especially basketball. I had the opportunity to play on my middle school and high school teams. My biggest fan was my mom. She came to every game, even the away games. One team we played had the scorer's table built into the bleachers. Our game was finished, and we were sitting in the bleachers watching our guys play. Mom had to go to the restroom and as she climbed down the bleachers, she grazed the score table and fell onto the court. The person sitting beside me asked if I was going to check on her. I told her I was in a minute. I was embarrassed, and I know she was even more so. I eventually went to check on her and she was okay.

Paul says in Romans, "I am not ashamed of the gospel..." How often am I embarrassed of being a Christian when others are making fun of me? We have no reason to be ashamed or embarrassed by Jesus or our life in Him. Boast

in Him. He is worth it, and He allowed himself
to be humiliated to have a relationship with
you.

Stormy Night

There is no fear in love. But perfect love drives out fear, because fear has to do with punishment. The one who fears is not made perfect in love. 1 John 4:18

The first night a child stays at home alone is both exciting and scary. My first night by myself was at my grandmother's lake house. My family went home, and my cousins were coming the following morning. I wasn't old enough to drive, so I was still fairly young. The lake house is an old house that makes lots of noises, especially at night. It's quiet down there, so you hear every little sound. That particular night, it began storming as I was watching television. A little scared already, I was on edge. Suddenly, the phone rang and scared me to death. Now, the phone at the lake was an old rotary phone and the volume was very loud, so we could hear it from the porch. There was no real danger there. The phone call was our neighbors who lived two houses down calling to check on me.

There are times in our lives when we are afraid of various things. We do need a healthy fear, so we don't do things that endanger our lives. But there are some fears that are unhealthy. I recently discovered I had a fear of people. I wasn't afraid of people physically harming me. Instead, I was afraid of letting others down. This affected me more than I knew. I felt responsible for people but learned that I'm not responsible for others. I'm responsible to others. This manifested in broken relationships, being used by others and a great deal of stress. I put so much pressure on myself that I was miserable. In high school, if I missed a shot in basketball, it would cause me much internal turmoil because I felt like I had let my team down.

God has taught me, and is still teaching me, that there is no fear in love. God loves me, and I could never let Him down. His love for me is perfect and unconditional. He loves me whether I make or miss the shot. He loves me when I fall in sin or succeed in resisting. He loves me even on the days I find it hard to love myself. Yes, I will let others down, but I have a God who continues to love me even though others may not. I am loved, redeemed and belong to Him. That's what matters in this life. If I rest in His love for me, what others think will not matter as much and I can live in freedom from stress and anxiety.

A Man in His Hammock

Come to me, all you who are weary and burdened, and I will give you rest.

Matthew 11:28

One picture that sticks in my mind as a child is my dad laying in the hammock. We had a rope hammock between two oak trees at the lake. He loved the hammock and always wanted it to be swinging. He tied a rope to the hammock and the other end to a nearby tree. Whenever he stopped swinging, he would give the rope a yank to continue swaying and eventually fall asleep.

Hammocks are a great place to rest. I recently bought one of my own and spend time resting in it at home and at the lake when I can. I'm not sure what makes it so easy to sleep in a hammock. Maybe it's the breeze blowing through the hammock or the sun warming my face as I listen to the sounds in nature.

As I've gotten older, I am realizing more and more the importance of good rest. Even the

Lord took time to rest physically, emotionally and spiritually when He walked this earth. If we don't rest, we won't have anything to serve others with. We can only give what we have received. Another important lesson is to give from the overflow. If we are constantly on empty, we will never have enough to give others. Stay filled up with Jesus by resting in Him.

Teamwork

We have different gifts, according to the grace given to each of us... Romans 12:3-8

When I was in college, I would often visit my Grandmother. She didn't live too far from Clemson and I enjoyed spending time with her. One Friday after classes, I decided I wanted to go to the lake so I stopped by her house to see if she wanted to go as well. She didn't have to think about it. She said, "Let me grab my bag." Yes, my eighty-something year old grandmother had a "go bag." She had a bag packed so she could go at a moment's notice.

We stopped by the store to buy some groceries and were on our way. The drive was approximately an hour from her house, so we had some good quality time in the car.

After unpacking the car, we walked down to the pier with rods, tackle and bait in hand. I think we both had a couple of rods baited with red worms. We hoped to catch enough for a meal. At one point, Grandmother had to go up to the house to get something and I caught a huge bluegill on her rod. I showed her the fish I had caught on her rod and she smiled. When another family member looked to see what we had caught, Grandmother said, "Look at this nice one Holly and I caught." She informed me since it was on her rod, that she had a part in the catch. I still smile when I think about that night.

In the Christian life, we need each other as well. We are in this race together and God created the body of Christ to need each other. We have been given different spiritual gifts which are all needed in the church. It doesn't matter which one catches the fish. We are all participants. One may have baited the hook and another casted the line so that you could catch the fish. God gives us tasks to do and we need each other. If you use the gift God has given you and your brothers and sisters use their gifts, you can accomplish more than you ever could on your own.

Rainstorm

He got up, rebuked the wind and said to the waves, "Quiet! Be Still." Then the wind died down and it was completely calm. Mark 4:39

There's something beautiful and awesome about watching a storm come across the lake. However, our perspective is a huge indicator as to our response to the storm. When I'm sitting on the porch, it can be so peaceful. However, if I'm in the boat, the peace can quickly become anxiety.

On one occasion, I was about 20 miles up the lake with my cousin and the rain was coming down hard. To make matters worse, it was late at night. We couldn't see our hands in front of our faces and we were getting hit with what felt like needles as we sped to the lake house. It was a little scary and we were both soaked.

This reminds me of times when the disciples were in a boat during a storm. Their boat was being overtaken by waves. They were terrified and asked Jesus to help them. He did above and beyond that. He calmed the storm with His voice. What power!!

He can do the same for the storms we encounter. In one word, He can calm the storm or give us peace during the storm. His control is limitless. Next time that storm surprises you, trust in the one who can calm the storm.

Hold Me Tight

He will feed His flock like a shepherd. He will carry the lambs in His arms, holding them close to His heart. He will gently lead the mother sheep with her young. Isaiah 40:11

When my nephew, Dawson, was three, I took him to his first Clemson football game. Already a huge fan, he was so excited to be there and was having a great time, but as the crowd increased in sized and proximity, he became scared. His words were simple, yet profound. "Hold me, Holly. Hold me tight." Of course, I wrapped my arms around him and held him close to my heart, and his fear diminished.

We all struggle with fear and insecurity at times, and the "fix" is so simple. "Hold me, Jesus. Hold me tight." He longs to comfort us and make us feel secure in His loving, powerful arms as He holds us close to His heart. As we feel His heartbeat, our fears and insecurities will decrease. Next time, the worries of this life begin crowding us and beating us down, call out to the only One who can calm our fears and give us perfect peace. HOLD ME, JESUS. HOLD ME TIGHT!

Heaven

We are confident, I say, and would prefer to be away from the body and at home with the Lord. 2 Corinthians 5:8

My father passed away in 2009 from a short battle with pancreatic cancer. My nephews were young and didn't understand what was happening. All they knew was that Pa Pa was going to heaven.

After Dad passed away my brother wanted Daddy's truck. Mom and I took it to his house, and I'll never forget what little Thomas said. He walked out on the porch and said, "Is Pa Pa already back from heaven?" He associated that little red truck with his Pa Pa and thought he was back from his trip to heaven.

Death can be very hard and very confusing for us. We can't fully comprehend what takes place at that moment of death, but we know that our loved ones are in the presence of God forevermore if they knew Him. This being said, no one who is in His presence would want to come back here. His presence is a place filled with love, joy and peace. We long for that kind

of life here on earth, but it will never be fully
realized until we are in heaven with our Lord.

Gone

And just as each person is destined to die once and after that comes judgment. **Hebrews 9:27**

December 13th is a day that will forever be etched in my memory. It was a normal day and I had errands to run before the basketball game that evening. On my way home, I was met by my mother's friends at the stop sign. They asked if I was going home and turned around and followed me. As I pulled into the drive, cars were parked everywhere. My dad was even home from work. I knew something was wrong, but nothing could have prepared me for the words that Dad met me at the door with... "Grandmother's GONE."

I was speechless and remember leaving the house on my bike and riding so hard. I didn't know how to begin to deal with my Grandmother being GONE. She was my rock. We enjoyed the same things and had similar personalities. I had just spent the day with her the day before. Mom and I drove down to go shopping with her, and now I cherish that day that the Lord gave me with her. I'll never forget that day.

Mom, Dad and I packed and drove to Williamston to be with the rest of the family. I remember Freddy coming up to me and hugging me telling me how much Grandmother loved me. I knew she did. The way she bragged on me was so cute. She would put my volleyball picture in her wallet so that when she wrote a check people would see it. Then she would proceed to tell them, "That's my granddaughter, Holly, she goes to Clemson College.'" She said it with such pride. I loved her so much.

When Grandmother would go places, she would write where she was going on a dry erase board in the kitchen so that we would know where she was if we came to visit. It would say things like: "Gone to Anderson" or "Gone to the lake." On the 13th, the board simply read "GONE." There was nothing else on the board.

It was such an eerie feeling, almost like she knew she was leaving for good. She had truly gone home to a place with no pain or sorrow. She was and is face to face with our Lord Jesus.

One day, our imaginary dry erase board will read "GONE." To be blunt, it will read one of two things. For those of us who have accepted Jesus as our Lord and Savior, it will read "Gone Home to be with Jesus." For those who have never made that commitment, it will read "Gone, eternally separated from God in Hell." What will your dry erase board read on that day?